Soft Spoken

Soft Spoken

(Emotional words guaranteed to heal your heart, massage your mind, and stimulate your soul0

Soft Spoken

All Rights Reserved.

Copyright 2007 by Tiffany J McDonald

No parts of this book may be reproduced or transmitted in any form or by any means, graphic, electronic, or mechanical, including photocopying, recording, taping or by any information storage retrieval system, without the written permission of the publisher/author.

Printed by LuLu and 48 Hr Books
Published by Free2BInspyred

ISBN: 978-0-6151-7436-5

For speaking engagements and booking, open mic events, contact

Tiffany J McDonald

Soft_spoken_07@hotmail.com

http://www.myspace.com/soft_spoken_07

Soft Spoken

Dedication

To my daughter, Kambria Kaimille Stradford ....Mommy love you always and forever!!!

To all the poetry lovers that enjoy reading poetry

To all the women (and men) that need healing in their heart, to massage their mind, and stimulate their soul.

Soft Spoken

Soft Spoken

Acknowledgements

To my Lord and Savior, Jesus Christ for giving me this gift of writing and the ability to express myself with words.

Thank you to all my family and friends for all of your encouragement, love, and support. I could have accomplished my dreams without your love. I love you al!!!

Soft Spoken

Note to the Reader

Dear Reader,

Thank you for purchasing this book!! Your support is greatly appreciated!

You are about to embark on a journey of happiness, joys, tears, fears, heartache, heartbreak, love, loss, pain, abuse, misused, and erotic, intimate passion.

The words that are in this book are all original and filled with intense emotion. It may get a little heated at times.....so if you can't take the heat...."get out of the kitchen".

This is my "emotional therapy session" ; my venting place; my place where I am able to turn when there is no where to turn. You are about to understand the true meaning of "Soft Spoken" and why she is "Inspired".

Once you read this book....please provide your feedback/comments/testimonies....I would love to know how I helped

- **To Heal your Heart**
- **To Massage your Mind** *and*
- **To Stimulate your Soul!!*

Happy Reading!!

Soft Spoken

Parental Warning: There may be some explicit language and/or descriptive sexual acts, which may be inappropriate for any persons under age 18.

Read with caution!!!

"I don't just write poetry; I speak from reality!"

--Tiffany J McDonald

Soft Spoken

"Whispering to your Soul...."

"Hurt By Love"	11
"Love's Defeat"	12-13
"My House is not your Home!"	14
"Love Letters"	15
"The Poem without Words"	16-17
"Intimate Verses"	18-19
"The Pain that Never Goes Away"	20-21
"Wandering Eyes"	22
"Five Minutes of Computer Love"	23
"Letter to Soul"	24
"Giving Me the Cold Shoulder"	25-26
"Fulfillment of a Void"	27
"Freestyle #1"	28
"A Distant Memory"	29-30
"A Girls Confession"	31
"Torn Apart by Prison Doors"	32-33
"Words Overpowering the Body"	34-35
"So Hard to let Go"	36-37

Soft Spoken

"Chocolate Suga" 38

"The Tru Essence of a Woman" 39

"Back in the Day" 40-41

"Learning to Love" 42-43

"Intimidation" 44-45

Soft Spoken

Hurt By Love

The past hurt has overwhelmed my heart, it has consumed me…taken over my body
Broke those chains …those ties…the bonds of love
I want to love you and give you my heart and my soul, but how do you love someone that don't want to love you back?
It was magical, it was happiness, the life that we lived, it all soon changed, you flipped the script,
Showed your true colors because …I had your baby…got a better job and…you were jealous;
Yes, jealous…because you were not the center of attention. It was not about you…get this, a grown man carrying on like a child…what a shame!!
My heart is bruised, torn, scraped, and punctured….the hurt you have caused you don't even realize,
But you don't care and you say you love me; or are you saying that because it sounds good,
Why did you marry me? Was it just for show…to show that you are a man when you are really a little boy
Where is the love?? I want it to be there…I want to be a family…..
But….
I can't…you don't really want love. You enjoy the idea of love but not the responsibility
I can't take all this misery and pain; it is always zero losses and more gains,
You are hurting me , killing me and you don't even know it.
You want me to kiss your ass and not say a thing and that's not what I'm going to do….
I would rather be by myself than to be with you!!!

Soft Spoken

Love's Defeat

I've been defeated…I've lost the battle, the war;
it was a horrifying event, I can't even mention the score.
Left me with a feeling of embarrassment and stupidity….i feel humiliated!!
I've been beaten…by the game I know too well,
Torn apart in every which way your heart could be torn,
Scorned for life …don't know if I will be able to find a way to heal my internal damage.
The pain that was caused…I'm broken, it hurts…how could the one cared so much cause so much pain?
Was it all in vain??
Was he living a lie??
I've been defeated…defeated 24 to O,
Not even coming close…I'm tired of losing the battle my family and friends have won,
I want to just throw in the towel and say,
"I'm done!! I quit!!" ; but…I can't I won't…
I want to stick it out and hang in there, but every time….
I am defeated!!
Tears run down my face, causing more misery and pain to my life,
My self-esteem continues to lowers, allowing me to feel sorry for myself
Is it really me??? Is it something within me???
What am I doing wrong???
Damn…I tired of singing the same song! Its not meant for me…I'm not supposed to be blessed with a man,
I guess the single life is the way I'm supposed to go…which is what I don't want.
I don't want to live alone nor sleep in a cold bed,
I don't want my daughter to grow up without a dad or have a part-time dad,

Soft Spoken

I want to have a family o f my own; I want to have my own place to call home……
I want the heart, I want love…but unfortunately……
Love has defeated me!!

Soft Spoken

My House is not your Home!

My heart is not a revolving door, coming in and out as you please.
You're not loving me, your hurting me….
The pain is killing me on the inside, tearing me apart and causing me to bleed every damn time you leave…..
And leave….and please, don't leave…unless you are not happy here ,
Only putting up with me , stringing me along for the ride
No I am not your damn charity case or a lonely child that should be felt sorry for
I am a grown ass woman with a beautiful little girl to care for, you say yourself,
"this house is not a home…your home"
So where is home??? Home should be where your heart is and your heart should be with me and your daughter
A house is a physical place where you reside,
A home is in your heart; it's the place you long for when away
Home gives you comfort and peace…day to day
Home is …Heart felt love that is openly honest and trust-worthy of each other,
Its memories of the good and bad times together,
Enduring the wonderful love you have together
Are you at home?????

Soft Spoken

Love Letters

Can I write you a love letter?
Can we write love letters to each other?
Letters that express our emotions, our gratitude toward one another,
Love letters tell each other about their day, the problems we encountered
And how much we missed each other
I want a love letter from you…I've sent many to you,
And didn't get a response….did they get lost in the mail?
Maybe it was the wrong address, so It didn't know where to go
I want to receive a love letter from you,
So I can feel you through the words on the paper,
My emotions will take over my body, as the words become real
I want to hear your voice echo as I read the words
I just want you…in more ways than one, wanting to make love to you
again
Oh how I miss that…the way you and I move, we make swift music, as
we dance to our own beat
My love letter and your love letter together brings enchanted love to life
So can I write you a love letter?
Or we can write love letters to each other,
Our hearts will open up and the words will just flow…flow heavenly and
gracefully like the Mississippi River
Love …a beautiful thing and shall never be taken for granted
Can I write you a love letter?
Can we write love letters to each other?
And let the entire world know our story of love

Soft Spoken

The Poem without Words

I want to write a poem,
A poem you've never read or heard before
I want to speak to your mind.
Challenge the way you see things from another point of view
I want to talk to your heart,
Spread my feelings out all around you, so you can grab and hold on tight
My inner voice…the poet's voice….the writer inside….
Wants to come out and play
She wants to be friends and lovers in a special unique way
A bond is what she wants, closeness…intimate relationship with her mate
I want to write a poem,
Tell you about my day, not a complaint ever involved
Just what's on my heart so there are no secrets that bring us apart
I just want to talk and learn to listen, too
You mean the world to me , you are my boo,
Maybe you should write me a poem or a letter or two
Allow me to get inside you so we can talk with each other, not just
tolerate each other , but love one another
I wanted to write you a poem, one you never heard before
New style, fresh ideas….words that are real
I didn't want to write to preach,
Or to make is seem like a know it all; I didn't want to try to cover up my
feelings,
I wanted to write a poem that came from deep down inside, writing
without any cares or any feelings to hide
I didn't have do much thinking, just let my pen do the work and my mind
flow
The words, ideas and structure come together on their own
But with my help it has grown from a baby sentence into an adult poem
The maturity level sky-rocketed and will continue to grow

Soft Spoken

I want to write a poem
I want to change my style
I want to talk to you
But…..How when the words just won't come out???

Soft Spoken

Intimate Verses

I saw you and you spoke to me with those words
Listening to your every word, watching your every movement
From the head wrap on your head to the brown boots on your feet
Immediately you locked me into a state of mind…an intimate poetic state
Words…..
Yea, your words, were real and captivating
Makes me want to make poetry love
Using the power of my pen to write you to me
Line by line
Stroke by stroke
Mesmerized….Hypnotized….
anMakes me realize the "true" meaning of poetry
Sweet……sensual…..
Passionate….wet……sexual kisses…….
Those kisses that allow me to meet and become yours
Running your tongue from my lips all the way down to my stomach and below, spelling out,
i-love-you
punctuate….while you take me on a ride,
a ride to the Promised Land, a ride to the forbidden poetry island where we can stimulate each other
and have the "Greatest Sex" ever
I'll "strip for you" down to the red lace Victoria Secret and "you won't be saying no tonite"
12 ways
12 hours
Just me and you
Those words, your words….beautiful
Elevate my mind
Stimulate my soul

Soft Spoken

Mend my heart
You are just so "Nice"
Can't wait to hear you read, read to me
Read me to sleep
Make poetry love
And turn me on ….I mean; turn me into your poem
Two poetic intelligent minds
Coming straight from the "Land"
Equals
One body, one soul, one creation

Soft Spoken

<u>The Pain that Never goes away</u>

Look
Look into my eyes
In order to feel what I feel,
Know what I know
Cry what I cry
Love what I love
Look
Just look at me
And see the pain that's hurting deep down inside
Smiling and laughing
Just to keep from crying
It hurts and….
No one understands
No one knows

I just can't understand
Just can't tell you why some act the way they do
Is it real??
What did I do??
I try my hardest to be friendly and nice
I don't cop an attitude
Unless…….
You come at me the wrong way
Hearing the whispers, the snick ling, the giggles
My conscience starts to feel guilty, guilty of whatever it may be
Can we just pause or rewind, stop and play again
Or how about feel me in???
Nope sorry , just can't do….
Cause its all about you, who? Me!
So ….

Soft Spoken

Look….Look into my eyes
In order to feel what I feel
Know what I know
Cry what I cry
Love what I love

Heal my broken heart ,
My troubled times
And ease the pain away
For I am drifting…..drifting……drifting……astray

Soft Spoken

Wandering Eyes

My eyes are seeing something that my mind is trying not to,
Trying not to like you since I "will never have you"
But my eyes are noticing your body, your looks, your personality
Those hugs are my weakness who could ever resist
You take me……
You move me……
I want you!!!
But the question is still in mind
Can I have you???
Can I ….have you….???
Even though I have a boyfriend or even though girls be on you like glue
You are just a flirt, a ladies man…one day I will be this man's lady
Secretly…..
Telling you that I like you and that I want to be with you,
Can you hear me???
As I whisper through this computer,
The softness of the keys as I talk, and quietly I end by hitting send
Did u hear me???
Did u listen???
What is your answer???
Feel like I am back in elementary school…..
Check yes, no , maybe
But I am all grown up and my eyes….
My beautiful brown eyes are seeing a beautiful brown man
That my mind is trying not to focus on and those eyes continue to ask the question….
"can I have you?"
A question of truth
A movement of reality

Soft Spoken

Five Minutes of Computer Love

In walks a cool, laid back, real nigga,
That nigga that I been on for a while,
Trying not to lust after you, crush after you cause I know I can't have you
STOP!!!
Stop doing this to me, you know???
Getting to me like this…..
U don't even have to say a word
Its your physique
Your style
Your charm
You are my playboy, my love toy…
In my mind
Saw you playing basketball the other day….damn!!!
Can I be your shorts that day?
That nice round booty, I just want to grab and never let go
Sweat all running down your body…come over to my room….618
And we'll be sweating alright…..sweating with the juices of love
Leaving the room…all I hear you say, "see you later"
Really???
Later???
Later in my room….my dream has come true
I WISH!!!
STOP??
Please…stop doing this to me,
This cool…laid back…real nigga
That I am trying not to lust after, crush after
Cause I already know I can't have you

Soft Spoken

Letter to Soul

Dear soul,
You left me or maybe misplaced me
Or even ran away from me.
Here I am standing all alone, have no home
Or no one to call my own.
You left me…
Hanging out to dry…..Why??????

Did you get scared when your "mate" left you?
So u just said, "I'll run and hide"
Not even caring what was in my mind
You blew me off with no type of explanation
And now we can't even start procreation…that little bundle of joy…
Her name….Love
I am so lost and have no where to go, no where to turn
Hope this finds you well and you see the pain that I'm going through
And maybe I'll be able to find you
Always and Forever,
Heart

Soft Spoken

Giving me the Cold Shoulder

Brrrr!!
Its freezing , freezing cold
Cause I feel a draft of the cold shoulder coming on strong
Harsh words coming towards me
Like a bullet with no name
And a person with extremely good aim
BANG!!!
Shot me right in the heart,
Bleeding with tears and those harsh words
Sentences, phrases
Are hurting my ears
What is wrong??
What is the matter??
Whatever happened to us laughing,
Smiling and feeling overcome with joy?
Is it because I said u were acting like a little boy??
Its true., in more ways than one
You playing these games like I'm the mother and you are my son
Can we go back to the good ol' days where you were talking about us
And not even making a fuss??
I just don't get it ,
U flipped ever since u sent it….sent it to early, I guess
Got backed in a corner , so now you come out fighting
But why me??
Why am I the opponent, the enemy at hand???
I thought I was your girl and you were my man???
Things changing now, getting closer and closer to a date
Maybe I was the one who made the mistake,
made a big mistake of pouring my heart to you , coming on too strong
HA! I guess I am the one looking like a fool,

Soft Spoken

" A fool who thought she was in love"
Brrr!!!
Its really freezing, freezing cold
Cause I feel the draft of the cold shoulder coming on strong
My heart still feels for you
Even if yours doesn't feel it too
My love is real and comes from deep down within
Soon your love will be real…when I win!!!
Till then…..I …..am….
Freezing, freezing cold
Cause I feel the draft of the cold shoulder coming on strong
Brrrr!!!!!!!!!!!!

Soft Spoken

Fulfillment of a Void

This feeling
This need
This want…..is nothing but a fulfillment
Filling up the empty space that is left in my heart, its so hollow
I can hear its echo
Seeing your face, your physique, I can't help but stare
Don't want to seem obvious
So I can catch myself and take a peek out of the corner of my eye
Admiring you in that tight black muscle shirt
Showing off those arms…..
Yea , I want to feel those arms around my body,
The warmth
The closeness
Your companionship is the most I want
Bringing out the shy girl in me
Afraid to say too much
Afraid of pouring out my heart
And never being apart of you
Bringing back elementary school days,
"can u tell him?"
How old am I ??
But…..
I know what this is ,
I know why ,
This feeling
This need
This want
Has completely taken over my body
Its trying to bring something back that isn't there
Trying to fulfill a void that has left my heart

Soft Spoken

Freestyle #1

feel my lips touch against yours
soft
feel our tongues together
sensational
feel the warmth of our bodies together
wonderful

two African American bodies together,
male and female, uniting as one

feel the touch of your hands caressing my body
don't stop!
Feel the touch of my hands caressing your body
delightful
stimulated not by your body, which is beautiful
but...
Stimulated by your mind...
A mind that knows where to go in life
look into my eyes and see...
You plus me, growing together in all eternity

Soft Spoken

Distant Memory
(Dedicated to the victims of Hurricane Katrina)

In a blink of an eye…in a moment of time,
In a flash of a light…one moment…one second…
Right before your eyes, your life rewinds your past, plays the present and fast forwards the future
And then ………GONE!
Its gone….like a thief in the night, just like that, everything you worked for, lived for, and hoped for….is now a distant memory.
A memory, your precious, fondest memories…your identity….your own story washed away forever
Who would have thought?
Who would have known…that when I went to sleep in my bed…
I would wake up with no home….no food….no job…no family……………..NO WORLD
My city has been destroyed; my life has been taking from me
Why should I continue to live?
Why should I continue to press on?
There's nothing to look forward to and nothing to live for,
There's nothing to motivate me.
My head is hung low and tears flow down my eyes
I can't even hear Maya Angelou speak, "Rise child, Rise"
And I want to stand up….I want to continue on with life, but how….how can I continue with only a distant memory???

My child, it may be a distant memory, and even though you are sad,
You are still a child of GOD and still need to smile with joy in your heart,
GOD will continue to love you and never part you.
At this moment, this time of despair, is the time you need to get on your knees and pray…
Pray that GOD will see you through the storm.

Soft Spoken

The storm will surely pass and at the end will be a rainbow… a rainbow full of a new life, a new beginning….a fresh start.
GOD does things for a reason and never makes a mistake.
GOD is a God of order and always comes on time,
 If you have and put faith in HIM…..the memories of your life won't have to be a distant memory.

Soft Spoken

A Girl's Confession

my mind,
my soul,
my heart quivers at the thought of me not being there with you.
i get these feelings inside me where i just can't stop thinking about you.
"Absence Make The Heart Grow Fonder", I hear people say all the time,
i am beginning to think: Could this be it? Could you...be...the one???

I sit and stare out my window for hours on end,
thinking and wishing you were here with me.
Watching the raindrops fal on the pavement and
i immediately drift off to a scene from Love Jones.
You and Me, in the rain, together, kissing passionately
Getting soaking wet from the rain
"Don't worry !!! I will protect you baby!" I hear you say.
If only ...if only life was like i dreamt it.

I need your company.
I need you to hold me in your arms and just tell me that everything is
going to be okay.
I want to feel your warmth body against mine and touch you sweetly,
slowly, and sexy.
I want our bodies to intertwine and become one.
I want you to elevate my mind, stimulate my body to a higher state.
I ...want...you!!
Could it... Could it be....us forever?????

Soft Spoken

Torn Apart by Prison Doors

My heart is torn, torn apart by these prison doors,
Cause I don't have you in my life,
I mean…what happened?
I thought I was your wife.
We been through it all,
The good….the bad….The happy…the sad….and now its all ending
Or should I say being put on hold.
You try to do what you think is best for me, which is to tell me to , "move on"
Cause you think there is someone out there who's better for me,
You don't want to hold me back from my dreams and living life to its fullest , your protecting my feelings and don't want me to get hurt
Your doing what's best cause you really care for me
But in reality…..your only making it worse and your only hurting yourself
I know shit is going through your mind and you need to take time to unwind, sort things through,
But I want you to know that I really , honestly, truly love and miss you
You're my sun in the morning and my moon at night,
I wish I can just hear your voice so I can be able to sleep tonite
I've been tossin and turin' cause my body is yearnin'…and longing for you….
Can't you understand that my love is so forever true
It has taken me a while to write what I am feeling,
There's so much that I have been dealing
I wish things could go back to they were, the way my life used to be,
I just want to turn back the hands of time and stop all this speaking in rhyme
I want us to be together, live life to the fullest and be together until eternity.
You are and still is my best friend , always, forever and til the end.

Soft Spoken

I have given you my love, my time, my support, and my heart; so its kind of hard to separate and part.
But I will try to respect your wishes and give you this space,
And maybe it will help bring us closer and closer , and face to face
So my heart still stays torn….torn apart by prison doors.

Soft Spoken

Wordz Overpowering the Body

The power of words are strong,
A strong force that is weakening my body
I can't seem to pull away because I have found love in your poetry,
Or should I say your poetry has found the love inside of me……

I am really feeling you, digging you and forever lovin' your style
Even though I have only know you for such a short while
I can't seem to get you off my mind,
I have been captured and hypnotized by K's rhyme….
Chaos is how my heart feels at this moment, feelings flowing and moving in every direction and I don't know where to turn
Hearing you speak , its like you are speaking to me, melting my heart with your words and your animosity
Can I be the pen in your hands???
You can hold me and take me on a distant land, a land where its just us
…"free-flowing"
Using our tongues to create a sweet and sensual verse,
Can I be the notebook where all your thoughts lie??
Lay your head on my chest, as I began to caress and read between the lines. In order to find the "hidden" meaning of your "poetry"
I must first be interlocked with your mind, soul, and then your body
There it goes….you got me!! You got me writing like this,
My writing has now become a strong and loveable poetry bliss
And when its all over….maybe we can end in a kiss…

The power of words are strong,
A strong force that is weakening my body
I can't seem to pull away because I have found love in your poetry,
Or should I say your poetry has found the love inside of me……

Soft Spoken

"She's sweet!" is what I hear someone tell me,
Those words came from your mouth,
Your lips the same one I want to kiss,
I want to taste and begin to embrace, never letting go , cause after just one
I would want more
Playing back in my mind, that Friday as we say goodbye,
I felt a tingling sensation going up my spine,
It was your lips touch against mine,
My cheek to be exact and you rubbed your hands along my bacl
Oh…,my….what am I supposed to do do??
You have a girl, so how can I possibly get with you??

The power of words are strong,
A strong force that is weakening my body
I can't seem to pull away because I have found love in your poetry,
Or should I say your poetry has found the love inside of me……
I have been overpowered once again by the words of such a dear friend,
This feeling is a little different, its more personal than mutual,
And maybe…just maybe…something might develop in the future

Soft Spoken

So Hard to Let Go

How can I let you go?
Why didn't you wanna stay?
It was the many trials that got in our way
Your were apart of me,
The words you spoke, I believed, you opened my eyes
And made me see the true meaning of love
You were my best friend, I want us to become that again
How can I let you go??
You're the realest nigga I will ever know

My heart still yearns for you ,
You were the one who was true,
True to yourself, true to the game of life
You were so true to me, your were calling me your wife
We were the Twins…Gemini Twins,
We had so much in common, you would have thought we were kin
It was love at first sight , that made connection between us tight
Falling in love with you, giving you my all,
I just knew you were the one God had called
But the devil suddenly got between us and tried to bring us down and make us hate each other
But we had GOD on our side and still loved one another
"you complete me…"
"I am not going anywhere"
Echoes through my mind,
I am continuously thinking about you all the time,
Can't believe you cut me off and told me it was over and done,
After all I was there for you, you and me having so much fun
My heart and soul burns deeply for the lighting of your flame,
It would still be lit , you would still be with me…..only if you hadn't got

Soft Spoken

        caught up in the game
Wanting to be hard , roll with your boys and trying to be a thug….Now
you sitting there thinking, "thugs get no love"
I was your good girl, your good Christian girl with long hair,
I was the one who was always there and would always be there

So how can I let you go??
Why didn't you wanna stay?
So many trials that got in your way
You became apart of me,
The words you spoke I believed
You opened my eyes to see the true meaning of love
You were my best friend…I want to become that again
I wanna hear from you, your voice, your words, anything you have to say
How can I let you go?
        You were the realest nigga I will ever know.

Soft Spoken

Chocolate Suga

Can I ask you a question:
WHEN DID YOU FALL IN LOVE WITH POETRY?
You are the inspiration, the result of God's creation,
A strong willed, goal oriented man with a tremendous master plan
I take a breath….
Letting my lungs exhale ,
As I wait for the love to prevail
There is a feeling that has taken over my body
It all started…..that day….that night….that magical 15th of August
The magnetic force of the room
Grabbed a hold of us and we were attracted to each other,
Magnetically, rhythmically, and instantly…we felt the vibe …the beat of the music and let our bodies intertwine
As I began to think…"I want you to be mine", grabbing on to you and never letting go,
I felt so in control
At the end of the night, the night I didn't want it to end,
But I smiled when you whispered,
"can I get your number? We need to do this again"
I railed off seven digits, in a sweet, sexy voice, sexy with a whisper because of all the noise
Walking out, I felt two hands up on my hip, and immediately wanted to do the dip…..
Dip into your pool of chocolate and take a swim in your chocolate love
My heart beats faster, every time I think of you and hear from you
After 3 months of you chasing, you have finally caught me
So can I ask you a question:
WHEN DID YOU FALL IN LOVE WITH LOVE?

Soft Spoken

The True of Essence of a Woman

Women…we are…strong willed,
Able to stand tall and hold her own
Independent, steady going through life's trials and tribulations teaching her to grown
Very diverse and takes on many forms,
Different sizes….different shapes…..different colors…..
Made from the image of man is how we were born
One might say she's very liberated….some might say she's too sophisticated,
But in all actuality, we're just doing our own thang cause we're so educated
Using our minds, not our bodies to sell ourselves,
Trying to make in this world without a man's help ,
Not to say we don't need you, cause we do……
We all want a man who love us unconditionally, look beyond the outer beauty and focus on inner beauty,
Get to know us for the person we are inside, learn where the feelings and emotions lie.
Its not about how fast she can shake her ass, its all about having class;
Sorry…we're not the hood rats, the chicken heads from up the street, running around with every guy they meet
Sorry…we don't have to have to have sex to be sexy and because we don't …doesn't mean we're preppy
We're black Queen's , princesses, and daughters of the Nile,;
We're Divas and God's own child; we're worth more than gold and more than what men treat us
We have a grateful , laid back presence …this is nothing but a woman's true essence.

Soft Spoken

Back in the Day

I remember…those were the days ..remember like they were yesterday…an African American girl growing up in East Cleveland
Playing outside all day long, but had to be home when the streetlights came on. Favorite games…
Red Light Green Light, Mother May I, take 10 gigantic steps , or What time is Mr Fox?
Or All time favorite game we all loved to play….hide and go seek, but for y'all little freaks out there…Hide and Go Get it, wouldn't even hide, just stand in the open talking about "Come and get me"
Oh, remember -- Bubble gum, bubble gum in the dish, how many pieces do you wish?
Always played school even when you just got out of school
Played house…making cake and pies out of sand and mud, using the flower buds as decorations,
Going to the corner store, getting bags full of candy……Now and Laters, Sour Powers, Lemonheads, Boston Baked Beans, Chico Sticks, Marshmallow Pies….
And those hot , sour pickles with the juice left in the bag….and let's not forget about our favorite drink…Kool aid…what flavor ….red
Running to your mom to get money for the ice cream truck, all the neighborhood kids looking and racing for the ice cream truck…sometimes being the oldest meant getting ice cream for all the little kids ….Bomb Pops, Nutty Butties, Ice cream sandwiches, banana pops, and watermelon pops
Listening to music on your boom box on the porch…bumping A, B, C; Immature, MoKenStef….Jodeci, Sir Mix a lot, Kriss Kross….the list goes on and on
Yeah, those were the days….childhood memories……
Boys on the streets, playing football….sweating hard and looking good, Girls playing jump rope…Mabel, Mabel….Teddy Bear, Teddy Bear….

Soft Spoken

Watching Sesame Street where you learned everything…..from Spanish to counting with 'The Count , Mister Rodgers, Capt. Kangeroo, Muppet babies, Fraggle Rock
Those were the days, memories….I remember….back in the day

Soft Spoken

Learning to Love

hearing your voice on the other end of the phone
my heart starts to beat faster and faster .....
my mind wanders uncontrollable thoughts and desires,
i soon realize how much i love you
my love for you is greater than any other
your my best friend, my soul mate, my lover
your hugs are stronger than steel
and warm like a bear
your kisses are sweeter than honey
and worth more than any amount of money
through all of arguments , fuss, and fights
and through the many nights of crying tears of hurt and pain
i continue to look to the Lord and think with a positive head
that everything is going to be alright.
i miss you....
its only been two days, 1 hour, and 30 seconds
but....
you still have an effect on me every time i see you
my knees get weak,
my hands get sweaty
my body becomes hot and heavy
i hate it when we fight.....or when we argue,
i can't stay mad at you ....
because i love you
you are my Superman...
coming to my rescue,
saving me from all the hurt and pain,
filling the void in my heart that was once lost
you put in work and paid the cost

Soft Spoken

i am forever your Pooh Bear,
always got your back,
will love you unconditionally

hopefully this time and space will help us both
to learn , grow, and appreciate each other.

Soft Spoken

__Intimidation__

the baby that weighed into this world at 2 pounds 10 ounces,
so fragile and little ....and needed to be handled with care
the little girl with the round glasses and the pretty long hair
the teenager that was very actively involved but not actively popular
the adult that is career minded, goal oriented, and well established
lets her mind wander amongst her thoughts
ponder on life's questions
and starts to realize....
Men are intimidated by her success
I'm only five feet two,
but I have a big heart
looking and searching for someone to love me for me ,
romance me
and share a family with me
is it too much to ask??
am I being too selective??
or maybe not selective enough
I can lose my baby weight
and get rid of the glasses
I could add a little more chest and little more behind
but
that still wouldn't change my self being
I am still going to be me....
the woman .....the professional....
the one that men gets intimidated by her success
sorry.....men... I am not the trick that shakes her ass just to "get them dollas"
I don't have to sell myself for sex or lower my integrity
sorry....men.....I am not the gold digging type , who gets caught up in the "bling bling" hype

Soft Spoken

i only have one beautiful little girl, who is the love of my life.....and only one baby daddy....due to a mistake in my life

sorry...men....i don't get down on the first night ......and i am not here for the booty call or the one quick fix
i am just an intelligent , sophisticated African American woman
trying to relax and not be so uptight in this world called Life
Graduated high school and college with a higher degree
and established myself with high entry level career
maintained a level of dignity and do not have to act ignorant just to get noticed
so ....
until the end of time....
i will be the baby weighing in this world at 2 pounds 10 ounces ,
so fragile she had to be handled with care
the little girl with the round glasses and the pretty long hair
the teenager that was very actively involved but not actively popular
the adult that is career minded, goal oriented, and well established
waiting to on the Lord to see what HE brings in my life
and as men come and go....i will surely know .....
that little boys are intimidated by my success and real men congratulate my success
So...tell.....me.......Men....which one are you???????

Soft Spoken

A Word of thanks....

Did you enjoy the book?? Did it inspire you?? Did it "heal your heart, massage your mind, stimulate your soul??

I want to hear from you....and know your thoughts/opinions/concerns....

visit www.myspace.com/soft_spoken_07 and leave me a comment about the book.

Thanks again for your support!!

Love Always,
Tiffany

Sneak Peek.....

The Eyes Speak Many Voices

"Look into my eyes to hear my story……..

(Coming Soon in 2008)

Soft Spoken

Emotional Separation Anxiety Attack

*Through the doors ..past the guard…it awaits me…
It controls me….unable to turn off the force and take off the chains,
Minds gets cloudy…brain doing flip-flops…stomach gets nauseated…
As the whirlwind of feelings surround me…
The mental and emotional state of mind one person goes through….
Is a life - changing ….transformation…evolution….rebirth experience,
Floating through the clouds, unable to see your path…but feeling the wrath and emptiness of your love…your heart…your soul*

*Strong feelings …my heart feels for you, can't seem to get you off the brain…
You are like my shield through this emotional rain…cover me , hold me, console me…love me like no other
Wishing you could do all that and more…but thoughts are soon shut out ,
As distance separates the emotional attachment being felt by two people
How can such an instant connection between two …a man and a woman….be so strong
Almost like I've known you for years…like we have shared tears and fears…but all we shared was a moment…a kiss…a night,
Damn!! It felt so right, but why all the confusion, the hesitation, the doubts….
Trust your heart…ur instincts…your mind, body, and soul
I am the one ….to have and to hold…
"distance still separates the emotional attachment being felt by two people"
Your voice is soothing to my little ears…u gave me intimacy through the phone…making love to my mind
Giving me mental orgasms of mental attraction …true feelings of loving you
I miss my daily doses of "medicine"…need to be taken care of…but how when distance separates the emotional attachment being felt between two people*

Soft Spoken

www.ingramcontent.com/pod-product-compliance
Lightning Source LLC
Chambersburg PA
CBHW031436040426
42444CB00006B/840